365
QUESTIONS
FOR
COUPLES

365
QUESTIONS
FOR
COUPLES

Dr. Michael J. Beck
Stanis Marusak Beck
Seanna Beck

Adams Media Corporation
Holbrook, Massachusetts

Dedication

for Rachel, who has all the answers

Published by
Adams Media Corporation
260 Center Street, Holbrook, MA 02343

ISBN: 1-58062-068-X

Printed in Canada.

J I H G F E D C B

Beck, Michael J.
365 questions for couples / by the Becks.
p.   cm.
Written by Michael J. Beck, Stanis Marusak Beck, and Seanna Beck
ISBN 1-58062-068-X
1. Man-woman relationships. 2. Questions and answers.
I. Beck, Stanis Marusak. II. Beck, Seanna. III. Title.
IV. Title: Three hundred sixty-five questions for couples.
       HQ801.B355   1999
       306.7—dc21   98-47859
                               CIP

This book is available at quantity discounts for bulk purchases.
For information, call 1-800-872-5627 (in Massachusetts, 781-767-8100).

Visit our home page at http://www.adamsmedia.com

Contents

Acknowledgments

We would like to thank the following people for helping and inspiring us to write *365 Questions for Couples*.

Thank you to all of the fine editors at Adams Media Corporation, particularly Anne Weaver, who helped to whip our questions into shape.

Dr. Beck sends thanks to the following people for guidance and support: Dr. Jacob Kesten, Father Murray, Ph.D, and Dr. Phyllis Meadow, both of my parents, and Stanis, Rachel, and Seanna, who inspired me to do my best.

Stanis Beck would also like to thank Stephen Andrew and Eva Marusak (my parents, who set the stage), sisters Karen and Evelyn (who shared it), Dr. Jacob Kesten (who reframed it), my children Seanna and Rachel, and husband Michael (who enlarged and enlivened it), and to the many clients who continue to refine it.

Seanna Beck gives thanks to Linda Nussbaum, Emily Rawlings, Jen Malloy, Jenn DeVan, Neal Agran, Shay McGillicuddy, Ted Kavner, and Josh Nicotra, the best friends in the world. Thanks to her sister, Ray. Of course, she gives love and kisses to Greg Garrison.

We all give our love and thanks to Perry Nelson, to Kay Godan, who takes care of us and keeps us in order, to Bree McNichol, and to all those who play elemental roles in our lives.

Introduction

Do you remember *The Newlywed Game,* that television show where couples attempted to answer questions about their spouses for cash prizes? Do you recall smirking at people who couldn't recall if their husband liked skiing or surfing, and wives who weren't sure about the color of their husband's eyes? Have you, yourself, considered how many things you don't know about the people you care about? Have you wondered why your partner doesn't ask you questions anymore? Do you ever wonder about your lover's first kiss, or their relationship to their mother? Do you wish your partner would inquire about your past? Certainly, there are questions waiting inside of you. Now it's time to ask.

Our society has something of an "in your face" attitude to it, and in this rare time in our social history previously established norms have been dismantled by the media, the educational systems, and even the government, allowing forums for more open discussion.

Unfortunately, too often these forums don't take place in the most important arenas—between friends, lovers, partners, and people who play critical roles in each others lives. The most basic question can probe the deepest facet of one's psyche. Simple inquiries can provide boundless insight into someone's emotions and feelings. The problem is, the questions just aren't asked. When was the last time you shared a dream, a memory, or a feeling with your partner? If it has been a while, it's time to get started.

Simply put, *365 Questions for Couples* will allow you to get closer to your partner. Find some quiet time and comfortable space and sit with this book. Make sure that you have privacy, and that the phone won't interrupt your answers. Flip through, and find a question that you've never asked before. We've developed our questions based roughly on the categories that we ask our clients to focus on in our therapy sessions, requesting that

they consider goals and fantasies, life
experiences and reflections, emotions, dreams, ideas and fantasies
about sex, memories of the past, and
feelings about their relationships —
both in general and with their
partner. These categories represent a
broad spectrum of situations and
ideas that most people don't stop to
consider during the course of a typical day and, when combined, will
enable you to gain a more complete
understanding of your partner. Of
course, you can bypass questions
that may be too tough, or are inap-
plicable, or just too personal.
Certainly, there are no "correct"
answers, nor are there any wrong
responses. You can tackle a couple

of questions, or stick to one for a long time. Our only rule is that you cannot ask a question that you refuse to answer yourself. In order to create a comfortable environment and a sense of security, one partner should never feel coerced into revealing more than the other.

In our busy world, emotional connections are buried under the pressures of daily life, closing lines of communication within families. Perhaps some of the questions will raise uncomfortable issues or memories. Some of our questions might cause disputes. Regardless, all of our questions will bring you closer to understanding the person with whom you share your time. People often remark that the best part of a relationship is the beginning, when a mutual interest is shared, and couples learn eagerly about each other's past. Our book will guide you back to that state, an at-home therapy session which will provide all participants with a link back to their relationship's roots. Now, on to the questions!

Our
Relationship

$\mathcal{D}$o you believe that I know myself well?

$\mathcal{W}$hat is your favorite thing about my personality?

$\mathcal{W}$hat, if anything, have you learned from me?

$\mathcal{I}$f you could plan a trip for us to any place in the world, where would you choose to take us?

$\mathcal{W}$hat is your favorite memory about our relationship?

$\mathcal{H}$ow does it make you feel when we fight?

How do you feel about therapy? Do you think it would be helpful to you? Do you think it could help me? Would you ever consider going to a couples therapist together?

What's your favorite outfit that I wear? What, in particular, do you like about the way this outfit looks?

*I*n what ways do you think I could make your life easier or more comfortable? What changes or adjustments would I have to make?

*W*hat, if anything, do you feel you need to sacrifice or compromise by being a part of our relationship?

*H*ow well do you think I handle myself when I'm in a crisis situation?

*D*o you think I manage problems in our relationship well?

*W*hat do you suggest I do in order to enjoy life more? Are there any changes you believe I could make?

$\mathscr{W}$hat do you suggest I do in order to better enjoy my career? Are there any changes you believe I could make?

$\mathscr{W}$hat, if anything, do you suggest I do in order to relax and enjoy our relationship more?

*A*re there any topics that you don't like to discuss with me? Why do these subjects make you uncomfortable? Can you discuss them more easily with other people?

*I*s there any topic about which you wish I was capable of speaking more openly and freely?

$\mathcal{T}$ell me what you found attractive about me when we first met. How has this evolved or changed since we first met?

$\mathcal{I}$n what areas do you think we need to improve our relationship? Do you believe these changes are possible, or do you think we will always struggle with these issues?

Are there any minor changes that I could make to my appearance to make myself more attractive?

Do you think I have a lot in common with other members of my family? Who do I most closely take after, and in which ways?

*W*hat would you say if you could only communicate one last sentence to me for the rest of eternity? What would you like me to say to you?

*H*ow do you feel our relationship helps and/or hinders the fulfillment of your goals?

*W*hat are your basic expectations of your partner?

*L*ist the five things you appreciate about me the best. Tell me the five things about me that annoy you the most.

*D*o you believe that we will have to work hard to make this relationship a success in the future, or do you think things will just fall into place for us?

$\mathscr{W}$hat is a personality trait of mine that you fear may cause problems in our relationship? What characteristic do you have that might have a similar effect?

$\mathscr{D}$o you feel comfortable enough to cry in front of me? Do you think you could cry *with* me? What effect would my crying have on you?

*I*s there anything about me
that reminds you of your
mother or father? Is there
anything about me that
reminds you of anyone from
your past, either past lovers
or close friends?

*W*hat similarities in our backgrounds do you think contribute to the strength of our relationship? What differences could potentially cause us problems? (i.e., values, religion, culture, tastes, siblings, interests, parental and familial experience, etc.)

Are there times when you'd rather be alone than with me? Under what circumstances do you feel this way?

Would you be happy if I began to develop my talents and interests more, even if it took time away from our relationship?

*W*hat would you do to save
our relationship if it was
failing? Would you try
therapy? Would you change
your lifestyle, or your personality? How much would
you be willing to change?

*D*o you believe that you
can occasionally tell how I'm
feeling based on my body
language? Which emotions
do you pick up from me
when I'm not speaking?

Do you believe that I succeed in my relationships with people? What relationships in my life are particularly strong, and where do my weaknesses show?

What are my talents? Do you feel that you share these skills? If not, are they skills that you wish you had?

*I*n what ways do you think
I can help you with the
problems or struggles in
your life? In what circumstances would you turn to
me for help with a problem?

*I*n what ways do you
believe you can help me to
become a better person?

How important do you think you are to me? Do you think my life would be equally happy and successful without you?

What do you like about my physical features? Is there one feature that you like best?

*I*s there anything that
I do that makes you feel
uncomfortable?

*A*m I usually able to read
and interpret the signals that
you send? Which ones do I
interpret correctly, and
where do I need work?

Would you be willing to adopt children if you or I were unable to have children of our own? Would you adopt even if we *could* have children? Would you prefer surrogate motherhood or fatherhood to adoption?

*W*ould you be able to take
separate vacations from me?
For example, if we had a
limited amount of money
and separate interests,
would you take a vacation
alone or would you like to
try and compromise?

*I*n which ways do you think
we are alike? How are we
different from each other?

*D*o you wish that we had more in common, or would you prefer that we had more differing interests?

*A*re there any books or movies that you think I should read or see? Why do you recommend it?

$\mathcal{D}$o you think you could tolerate it if we had completely opposite political stances? Are there any issues that you feel are particularly crucial?

$\mathcal{W}$here do you see our relationship going? Do you believe we have the strength to continue to grow? Do you have any fantasies about our future, either together or apart?

*I*f you were single, how would your life be different? How would you spend the time that we normally spend together?

Relationships
With Others

What are your thoughts on the ways your parents raised you? In which ways did your parents succeed, and where did they fail?

Would you like a relationship that is similar to your parent's relationship, or one which is drastically different?

*W*ere your parents able to
successfully work out their
problems? What were the
most problematic aspects of
their relationship? How did
they handle these issues?

*W*ho, if anyone, was in
control in your parents' relationship? Do you think the
partner who did not have
control resented the one
who did?

*I*n what ways did your parents' views on race affect your opinions? Do you believe you were raised with prejudice? If so, how have you overcome these ideas?

*A*re you more similar to your father or your mother? In which ways are you like either of them?

*W*hat negative things have
you learned from observing
the way your family relates
to each other?

*W*hat positive things have
you picked up from watching
your parents' relationship?

$\mathscr{D}$o your parents or your
family have any traditions?
Will you encourage your
children to carry these traditions on to their families?

$\mathscr{W}$hat is the most important
thing your father taught
you? What are some more
minor things that you
learned from him?

*W*hat significant lessons or skills have you learned from your mother? What are some more minor things that you've learned from her?

*D*o you believe one of your parents loved you more than the other?

How did your parents discipline you when you misbehaved? Do you agree with their methods? What are your ideas regarding disciplining children?

Are you jealous of any of the members of your family? What makes you jealous, and why?

How do you plan to take care of your relatives when they are elderly? What do you think about nursing homes? Would you go to a nursing home in your old age?

*I*f you have siblings, how do you characterize your relationships with them? Do you believe that birth order was an important element in the development of your personality? If so, in what way?

*I*f you could leave behind one bit of advice for your children or relatives, what would you tell them?

*W*ho do you consider to be your best friend at the moment? Why is this person special to you?

*W*hat qualities do you seek in a friend? Which of your friends hold these qualities?

Are you envious of anything that one of your friends has? Is there any way you could obtain this same thing?

Who do you consider to be your most successful friend? In which ways has this person found success? Do you wish you were comparably successful?

What have you learned from your friends? Are there any ways you wish you were more like them? Are there ways that you're happy you're different from them?

Is there anyone who you believe you can trust to give you an honest evaluation when you go to them with a problem? Why do you trust this person, and what advice, if any, have they given you?

Do you maintain friendly relations with your ex-lovers?

*H*ave you ever been dumped? How did you get over the pain this caused you?

*W*hat is the craziest thing you've ever done for someone you love?

*D*o you believe the adage "absence makes the heart grow fonder?" What experience have you had with this?

$\mathscr{D}$o you look for relationships with people who are similar to you, or are you more attracted to opposites?

$\mathscr{H}$ave you ever had a relationship that you now wish you were never involved in?

$\mathscr{W}$hat is the worst thing a lover has ever done to you?

Do you believe that people who truly love each other never fight?

If you were single and lonely, what sort of initiatives would you take to seek out a partner?

How do you define a good relationship?

Have you ever played games to win someone's affection?

What qualities does a person have to have in order for you to trust in them?

$\mathcal{D}$o you believe that people who love each other should be completely honest at all times? If not, give an example of an appropriate time for concealing or bending the truth.

$\mathcal{I}$f trust is broken in an intimate relationship with you, can it ever be recovered? Have you had an experience with this in your life?

$\mathscr{D}$o you believe that both partners hold some responsibility for all problems in a relationship? Have you ever been in a situation where you felt the other person was entirely to blame for the problems? Have you ever blamed yourself alone?

*W*as there a specific moment when you realized that you are emotionally connected to me? What are your memories of that occasion?

*C*an you imagine giving up your present life for someone or something? For example, would you move to a distant country for true love? Would you leave your home and your friends for the perfect job in another part of the world?

*I*f you were to write a personal ad about yourself, how would it read?

$\mathcal{D}$o you think you have any physical flaws? What are they?

$\mathcal{W}$hat's the worst thing you've ever done to gain the approval or acceptance of others? (You might have to think back to high school for this one!)

$\mathcal{D}$o you think you are competent in standing up for what you believe in? In what circumstances have you done so, and when have you failed?

$\mathcal{W}$hat was the best cry you've ever had? Did you cry to someone else, or were you alone?

$\mathcal{W}$hat qualities do you hope your children will possess?

Emotions
and Dreams

Have you ever thought that you were going crazy or about to lose total control of your actions?

What is your greatest fear? Has it ever embarrassed you or scared you to tears?

*D*o you ever hear your inner voice saying positive or negative things to you? In what situations?

*T*ell me about a time when your anger caused you to be destructive. What did it cause you to damage?

When have you felt violated, be it your personal space or your trust? How did this manifest and how (if ever) did you overcome this emotion?

$\mathcal{D}$o you feel more comfortable in the city or in the country? What elements do you need in your environment to make you feel comfortable? For example, do you need to live near the sea to be happy, or do you prefer mountains?

*I*s there anyone in your life who has hurt you so badly that you can never forgive them? What were the circumstances of this?

*W*hat was the most frustrating experience you've ever had? How did you handle it?

$\mathcal{T}$ell me about a time in your life when you were moved to tears. How often do you cry?

$\mathcal{W}$hat makes you feel secure and safe?

$\mathcal{D}$o you feel that you understand yourself very well?

$\mathscr{D}$o you ever have any desires that you believe are silly or childish? Would you ever act on these wishes or desires?

$\mathscr{A}$re there any problems in your life that you believe you're not emotionally or physically ready to solve?

*H*ow do you think you deal with your anger? Do you handle it differently in different circumstances?

*H*ave you ever had a thought or feeling which could be dangerous if you acted on it?

$\mathscr{H}$ave you ever considered suicide? How do you feel about this, and what do you think of people who choose to take their own lives?

$\mathscr{W}$as there ever a time when you ignored your gut feelings about something? Was it the right thing to do? How did the situation turn out?

*A*re you comfortable
speaking in public? Would
you find it easier to speak to
a small group of friends, or a
large group of strangers?
What kind of experience
have you had with this?

*W*hen you get very upset,
do you ever have a physical
reaction? What happens?

Has your definition of love changed over time? How do you define love now, and how did you think of it before?

In your opinion, is it ever O.K. to express anger in a physical manner? In what circumstances?

*T*ell me about a time when you experienced a loss. How did you handle the pain this loss brought?

*D*o you trust yourself to respond effectively in an emergency situation? Have you ever been in the middle of a crisis? How did you handle it?

*H*ave you ever had an
animal that you loved die?
How did it make you feel?

*H*ave you ever felt
depressed? If so, what
brought these feelings on,
and how long did the feelings last?

How many people have you said "I love you" to? Have you ever changed your mind afterwards, or said it without meaning it?

$\mathcal{D}$o you think, at this point in your life, that you have the strength and emotional maturity to maintain a successful marriage? If so, when did you arrive at this point? If not, when do you suspect you'll get there?

$\mathcal{H}$ow do you feel about going to the doctor? Are there any illnesses that you fear in particular?

*A*re you scared of any animals? How have your feelings toward animals changed since you were younger? Do you remember a specific time when you felt scared of an animal as a child?

*D*o you think it is better to be controlled by logic and judgment or by emotions? Why?

Have you ever regretted a wish you made after it came true?

Have you ever regretted an action after observing how it affected someone?

Do you dream in color or black and white? Which colors do you recall as predominant in your dreams?

*D*o you ever daydream?
What's your favorite scenario?

*D*o you have any dreams
which repeat again and again?
How do these dreams evolve
over time? Do you like these
dreams, or do they bother you?

*H*ave you ever had one of
your actual, night-time dreams
come true?

$\mathscr{W}$hat is the worst night-
mare you've ever had? Did
you have this dream just one
time, or has it recurred?

 $\mathscr{H}$ave you ever learned
significant lessons or come
to conclusions about your
life based on dreams that
you've had?

Goals and Fantasies

*I*f you could have any experience right now, what would it be? If given the chance, would you choose an adventure like hang gliding, traveling the world, or skydiving? Or would you prefer an experience which expands your intellect in different ways, like learning a new language or seeing a play?

*I*f there was a play made based on your life, what would it be called? Would it be a drama, a musical, a comedy?

*W*hat did you wish for as a child? How have these hopes and wishes developed or changed? Should you have been more careful about what you wished for?

*W*hat is a talent that you wish you possessed?

*I*f you were given the opportunity to run for president, would you take it? If you won, what would you try to improve about our country?

*I*f you were selected to spend one year of your life volunteering at a charity organization, where would you choose to dedicate your time?

*I*f you were forced to change to a different career or field, what would you choose to pursue?

*I*f you could be famous for anything, what would you choose to be known for? Do you think you would enjoy fame, or would you detest the intrusion into your private life?

*I*f you could have just one wish granted today, what would it be? (You can't wish for more wishes!)

*T*ell me one of your personal goals for the future. What will you need to do in order to reach this goal?

*I*f you had to be either deaf, mute, or blind, what would you choose? Which would be the worst situation for you?

*I*f you could have any person who has ever lived at your deathbed to comfort you, who would you pick? Who would you like to have greet you first "on the other side," if there is such a place, and why?

If you were to get a tattoo, what design would you choose? How do you feel about the permanence of tattoos?

If you could make a permanent change to your body, what would you alter?

What role does money play in your life plans? How important will it be? How much money do you hope to make in the future? What (i.e., your time, your freedom) would you be willing to sacrifice to meet this goal?

After the basics (food, shelter, and clothing) what do you want to spend your money on in the future?

*I*f you could move to a city anywhere in the world, where would you choose to live?

*W*hat would your dream house look like, and where would it be?

*I*f you had to select three of your possessions to represent your personality, what would they be?

*W*hat's your favorite era in history? If you lived during this time, where would you live, who would you have liked to be, and how would you spend your time?

*I*f you had to teach a class on any topic, what would you prepare to lecture on?

*I*f you only had one more day left on earth, how would you spend it?

*I*f you had an entire day all
to yourself, to be spent
alone, what would you do?
Would you enjoy this experience, or would it make you
lonely? For how many hours
do you think you could
stand being alone?

*I*f you could be an expert
on any topic, what would
you choose to know about
and why?

*W*hat would you do if you lost your home and your belongings? If you could only save three things from the rubble, what would they be?

*I*f you were chosen to write and direct a movie, what would the plot be? Who would you cast? Where would you set it?

If you could choose the country of your birth, which country would you pick, and why?

If you could be reincarnated into another life form, what would you choose to be?

If space were not a consideration, what type of animals would you like to have, if any? How many pets would you like?

If there is such a thing as an afterlife, what do you hope yours is like?

*W*hat would you choose to do if you had an entire year to spend pursuing anything you wanted?

*I*f you could excel in one sport, what would you choose to star in?

*I*f all jobs paid the same, what profession would you choose to pursue?

*I*f you could be a super-
hero, what powers would
you like to possess?

*I*f you had to make a New
Year's resolution today, what
would you resolve to do?

*H*ow would you spend a
perfect summer day?

What artistic skill would you develop if you had the time and the finances to do so?

What do you imagine is the worst way to die? What is the easiest death that you can imagine? If you could choose, would you elect to die this way?

*I*f you were given $100,000 to invest in anything, where would you put the money?

*D*escribe how you'd spend the perfect day if money were not a concern.

*W*hat kind of car do you believe matches your personality?

*I*f you were provided with the money to start a business, what would you invest it in, and why?

*I*f you had the ability to do it without getting caught, would you steal a car for $100,000? Would you steal it for a million dollars?

Would you break into someone's home and steal a piece of expensive jewelry if it meant you would never have to worry about money again? Would you do it if it were the home of someone you knew?

*I*f you were given the money to throw a party for all of your friends, how would you go about putting it together? Where would you hold it, and what kind of theme, if any, would it have?

*I*f money were not an issue, would you undergo an operation to transform the features that you like the least about yourself? Why or why not?

*I*f you could live this life over again, what type of person would you try to be, and where would reside? Would you make the same decisions this time?

*I*f you could write a book, what topic would you write on? Would you choose to write a novel, or do you think you'd prefer to write a nonfiction book?

*W*hat dreams do you have for your children?

*Life
Experiences
and Beliefs*

What is your best quality?

What is your worst personality flaw? What sparks it?

What, in your opinion,
makes life worth living?

What would you like to leave behind when you die? Are there any special accomplishments that you hope to contribute to the world? What do you hope people remember about you when you've died?

Have you ever broken any rules in order to get what you wanted? Was it worth it?

*W*hat are your thoughts on gambling? If you found yourself in a casino, how much money would you allow yourself to spend?

*D*o you have any rituals in your daily life? Do you wish you had more?

$\mathcal{D}$o you like to dance? Is there ever a time when you won't dance, or when you definitely will? Do you dance at weddings, or at clubs? Do you have to drink to dance?

$\mathcal{W}$hat are your favorite things about your job? What's your favorite time during a typical work day?

Have you ever lent someone a large sum of money? Would you ever borrow a large amount of money from someone? Under what terms?

Has hard work ever *not* paid off for you?

*W*hat do you do to make
yourself look attractive?
When do you think you look
your best?

*W*hat is the best book
you've ever read? What
specifically about this book
moved you?

$\mathscr{D}$o you think the majority of people are kind and willing to lend a hand to someone who needs help, or do you believe that people basically just look out for themselves?

$\mathscr{D}$o you believe your astrological birth sign represents your character? What traits of your sign do you have?

$\mathcal{D}$o you believe that there are some things that, in general, men are better at than women? How about things that women are more successful at then men?

$\mathcal{I}$f it meant taking a 10 percent salary decrease, would you accept a job that truly offered you fulfillment? What if it were a 30 percent decrease?

*A*re you happier during any particular season of the year? Do you know why you like this particular season? What are childhood memories that you associate with this season?

*I*s there a place that you consider very meaningful? Why does this place play an important role in your life?

*H*ow important do you
think it is to have children?
Would you be willing to live
without being a parent?
Would you prefer it?

*D*o you prefer small gather-
ings or large parties? Has
your preference changed
over time?

$\mathcal{D}$o you have a favorite picture of yourself? Do you like this photo because of how you appear, or because it reminds you of a specific time or event in your life?

$\mathcal{W}$hat is the most important lesson you've learned in your life thus far?

$\mathcal{T}$ell me about a skill at
which you excel. How did
you learn this skill? Are
you proud that you have
this skill?

$\mathcal{D}$o you think it's more
important to be intellectually
smart or socially intelligent
in our society? If you could
only be one or the other,
which would you choose?

What do you like about
your physical features?

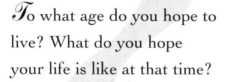

To what age do you hope to
live? What do you hope
your life is like at that time?

Do you feel that you live in
the present, or are you more
future-oriented or past-ori-
ented? Why do you choose
to focus your life in this
manner?

*D*o you believe in ghosts? Will you tell me your favorite ghost story?

*W*ould you describe yourself as a culinary adventurer, willing to try new and exotic foods, or are you drawn more to tried-and-true menus? What is the strangest food you've ever eaten?

At a gathering, do you prefer the attention of a crowd or would you rather speak one-on-one?

What's the biggest lie you've ever told? How did you feel afterwards, and what was the result of the lie?

Tell me about the best day you've had so far in your life. Describe your emotions throughout this day.

Do you believe that anyone can be bought at the right price?

Do you like your name?
Have you always felt this
way about it? If you could
change your name, what
name would you like to
be called?

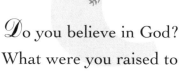

Do you believe in God?
What were you raised to
believe about religion?

*I*s a person's religion important to you when choosing a spouse or a partner? How could your partner's religion deter or encourage you in a relationship?

*W*hat do you think happens to us when we die?

What's the worst illness or injury you've ever had? How did you handle the pain this caused?

What is the best job you've ever had? Why did you like it?

*W*hat is the worst job experience you've had? Is there a job that was awful as a whole, or can you recall aspects of a job that you hated?

*T*ell me about the worst boss you've ever had. What qualities made this person difficult?

How do you feel about abortion? Are there times when either opinion could be objected to or condoned in your eyes?

How important do you think it is to conserve the environment?

How important is art in your life? Do you think your involvement with art is passive or active?

Do you believe in reincarnation? Have you ever had an experience that made you consider it as a possibility?

*I*s there anything that you fear you're too old to learn or to do? For example, do you think you are too old to go to medical school, or to skydive?

*W*hat were your talents as a child? Did your parents or friends encourage you to pursue these talents?

*W*hat is the biggest risk you've ever taken? Do you feel it was a wise risk to take and that it worked in your favor?

*H*ave you ever been involved in a situation in which you wished you could erase your actions? What did you learn from this experience?

What's the best class you've ever had? Why did you enjoy this class? Did the teacher contribute to your positive experience?

$\mathcal{D}$o you have any favorite
hobbies? Do you wish you
had more, or more time for
them? Do you prefer to
spend time on your hobbies
alone, or do you like working
with a partner? Are there
any hobbies that you think
we would enjoy sharing?

What is your most detested chore? Is there any way that this chore could be made easier on you?

Have you ever been in a hospital, either visiting someone or as a patient? What memories, smells, and sounds do you associate with the hospital?

*W*hat made you decide
to pursue your current
occupation?

*H*ow important is it to you
that others respect your
career? What did your
family think about the
career or jobs you've
chosen? How do you think
society views your career?

*W*hat is your personal definition of success? Do you consider yourself successful? What steps have you taken, or will you take, to reach your goals for success?

*T*ell me a trick that you've used to get something you wanted.

$\mathcal{T}$ell me your greatest
money-making scheme.
Would you ever like to
pursue it?

$\mathcal{W}$ould you ever own a
gun? If you do own a gun,
in what situations would you
use it?

$\mathcal{D}$o you believe that you have balance in your life? If so, how did you get to this point? If you believe you are still seeking balance, what efforts do you plan to make so that all your needs are met?

$\mathcal{W}$hat would be the ideal life for you in ten years? How about twenty years from now, and thirty?

*W*hat is the best vacation that you've ever taken? What made it so special?

*W*hat other careers have you considered pursuing in your life? Do you think you could be more fulfilled if you worked in a different field?

*H*ow do you feel about recreational drugs? Have you ever taken any? Would you try some if the opportunity arose?

*H*ow did your parents view drugs? Were their opinions typical or atypical of their generation?

What are you looking forward to in life? Are you excited about anything in the near future, or the distant future?

Memories

*W*ho did you play with as a young child? Tell me your favorite memory of this relationship.

*T*ell me about the best birthday you've ever had.

*H*ow did your childhood relationships change as you grew? Are there any child-hood friends with whom you still connect?

What was the biggest fight you've ever had in your life? Was this a physical fight, or an emotional battle? How did you resolve it?

Have you ever been unjustly accused of an act? How did you resolve the situation?

*D*id your parents love each other? How would you define their love?

*I*n what ways did your parents relationship succeed? What were its shortcomings?

How has your opinion of your body and your features evolved since you were a child? Do you remember your opinion of your physical features at different stages of your life?

What have you done in your life that makes you proud?

$\mathcal{D}$id you have a toy, doll, or blanket that you used for security as a child? What do you remember about it?

$\mathcal{A}$s a child, did you ever have an imaginary friend?

What was your favorite game during childhood? Did you ever create your own games, or did you play games that other children created?

Have you ever broken a law? If so, would you do it again? Are there any laws that you think are unfair, or made to be broken?

$\mathcal{T}$ell me about the first memory of your childhood that pops into your mind, no matter how simple.

$\mathcal{D}$o you have any special childhood memories of animals?

$\mathcal{W}$hat was the toughest subject for you in school? Why do you think you struggled with it? Do you like this topic now?

What is the hardest lesson you've had to learn outside of school? Have you struggled with something tangible, like learning a skill for your job, or have you had trouble with something less overt, like learning to share your emotions?

Are there any songs which evoke memories for you? What do these songs make you recall?

Are there any scents which remind you of the past? What memories do these scents recall for you?

*D*id you go to your prom? What was it like? Describe your date, and how you spent the evening. How did you end the night?

*W*hat is your favorite memory of high school?

*T*ell me about the absolute worst time you had during your adolescence.

*W*hat made you decide on the path you took after finishing high school? Were there any people who held an influential role in what you selected to do with your life at that stage?

*A*s a child, what did you want to be when you grew up?

What's the best gift you've ever received? How old were you when you received it? Why did it mean so much to you?

Search back through your memories and tell me about the one you believe is your earliest recollection.

*D*o you recall your parents fighting when you were a child? How did it make you feel to witness or overhear their arguments?

*A*s a child, do you feel you had a closer relationship with either your mother or your father? Did this relationship change or develop over time? Which of your parents do you feel closer to now?

When, if ever, was the first time you smoked a cigarette? What made you decide to try it?

Do you remember the first time you tasted alcohol? What was your reaction to it?

What did you do on weekends as a teenager?

*H*ow did your parents meet?

*H*ow old were your parents when they married? What details have you heard about their wedding day?

*W*hat was your favorite thing to do with your family when you were a child?

*W*hat's your favorite holiday? Why is this holiday special to you?

*T*ell me about a special experience that you had with a member of your family. Would you try to relive this experience again with your children or relatives?

*W*hat is the most embar-
rassing thing that has ever
happened to you?

*W*hen, in your life, were
you the most content? Did
you know at the time that
this was a special period, or
did you only realize this in
hindsight?

Have you ever performed
on a stage? Did you enjoy it,
and if the chance arose
would you do it again?

Tell me a story about one of
your grandparents. What
have you learned from them?

Tell me about the worst
date you've ever had. What
made it terrible?

$\mathcal{D}$o you own anything that evokes sentimental memories for you?

$\mathcal{W}$hat kind of monsters were you afraid of as a child?

What memories do you have of reading books with your parents or others as a child? Did you have a favorite book? What did you like about it in particular?

Tell me about the best date you've ever had. Why was this so special?

When you think of your mother during your childhood, what was her disposition like? Do you recall her being generally happy or often depressed? Did this change over time?

What is the craziest thing you ever did in your teen years?

*W*hat was your father's predominant mental state throughout your childhood? Do you recall a time when this affected you, either positively or negatively?

*T*ell me your favorite memory or story about one of your relatives.

If you were magically taken back to the first day of either high school or college, what would you do to make those years better for yourself? How would you change or adjust this experience?

Did you ever threaten to run away from home as a child? Did you put this threat into action? How did the situation end?

Have you ever been in a physical fight? What were the circumstances of this fight, and how did it end?

Tell me about a time when you felt left out of a group. What were the circumstances that made you feel like you weren't included?

*W*hat were holidays like
for you as a child? Which
ones meant the most?

*W*hat did your parents do
to help you enjoy life and
have fun when you were a
child? How did they try to
open your mind? How did
you respond?

Sex

*W*hat do you remember about your first date? Where did you go, and why did you pick this person?

*W*ho was the first person that you felt sexually attracted to? Do you recall what it was about this person that you were specifically attracted to? Did you act on this attraction, or keep it secret? Do you wish you'd handled the situation differently?

Who was your first sexual partner? Was your partner more experienced with sex than you were? What did you learn from this experience? Are you glad you chose this person to share your first time with you?

Do you prefer to be the pursuer in a relationship? Are you nervous when someone pursues you?

What is your earliest memory of anything having to do with sex?

Would you be willing to share your wildest sexual fantasy with me, even if I'm not a part of it?

*I*s there anything about sex that makes you feel awkward or uncomfortable, either physically or emotionally?

*I*f I suddenly lost interest in sex, would we be able to survive as a couple? How often do you think we need to have sex in order to have a healthy relationship?

*T*ell me about your first kiss. Was it a comfortable experience, or is it a bad memory?

*W*hat do you think the purpose of sex is?

*H*ave you ever been sexually attracted to one of your friends? Did you act on it?

*H*ave you ever seduced someone? Could you be seduced? How?

*H*ave you ever questioned your sexuality? Have you ever had a dream or fantasy about a member of your sex? How did this make you feel?

Tell me about the most consuming crush you've ever had. Was this focused on a person from your life, or a famous personality? What specifically made you fall for this person?

*W*ould you ever have sex with a person who was married to someone else? Why or why not? Would you ever consider having an affair with someone if you were married to someone else?

*H*ow did you learn about sex? What misconceptions did you have at first about this?

*H*ow often do you think a "normal" couple should have sex at our age? Do you think this should change over time?

*W*hat do you know about your parents' views on sex? How did they discuss the topic with you?

$\mathcal{T}$ell me about the sexiest dream you've ever had. Did you have this dream just one time, or has it recurred?

$\mathcal{W}$hat qualities do you find sexy in people that you're attracted to? Do you find these qualities in me?

*W*hat qualities do you find
attractive in members of
your own sex? Do you feel
you have these attributes, or
do you wish you did?

*W*hat do you think is the
sexiest part of the human
body? Is there any part of
my body that you particu-
larly like?

$\mathscr{D}$o you believe your parents had a normal, healthy sex life?

$\mathscr{W}$hat is your favorite part of sex? Do you enjoy the foreplay stage, or would you prefer to just "get down to business"?

$\mathscr{W}$hat is your favorite thing about having sex with me?

$\mathcal{D}$o you wish I did anything differently during sex? Is there anything I do that you don't enjoy, or that doesn't turn you on?

$\mathcal{H}$ow long do you usually date someone before having sex with them? Has this length of time changed as you've grown older?

*W*hat is your best sexual memory?

*D*o you think you've gotten better at having sex over time? What do you know to do now that you didn't know when you first started having sex?

What is your favorite kind of sex? For example, do you like having quick, athletic sex, or do you prefer long, slow sex? Describe your perfect sexual experience, from start to finish.

Have you ever had sex with someone that you didn't love? How does this experience differ from having sex with a loved one? Are there any benefits to having one night stands where you're unconnected emotionally to your partner?

$\mathscr{H}$ave you ever felt guilty about having sex? Why did you have these feelings, and how do you see the situation in retrospect?

$\mathscr{D}$o you feel comfortable discussing sex with me? Are you comfortable talking about it with your friends, or your parents? To what extent will you discuss sex with others—will you give details about your own sexual experiences, or do you just talk about it in vague terms?

Are there any specific scents that make you think about sex, or turn you on? Is there a reason that this scent peaks your interest in sex? What memories or feelings do you associate with this scent?

$\mathscr{D}$escribe your ideal sex life ten years from now. How much do you believe it will change from your current sex life? Do you believe you will learn more about sex over time and, as a result, become more experienced?

*W*ould you be willing to seek out new sexual experiences? For example, would you take a course on improving your sex life, or attend classes on tantric sex?

How important to you is communication during sex? Do you feel it's necessary to establish that your partner is being satisfied during and after the act? What do you say or do to make sure that you're fulfilling your partner's needs?

What part of sex do you think I enjoy the most? Is there anything special that you do that you think I particularly enjoy? Can you tell that I'm enjoying it from my facial expressions, or my comments?

Have you ever had sex with someone and regretted the experience? How did this make you feel? Did this influence your decisions on whether or not to have sex with someone in the future?

Would you ever have sex for money? How much would you demand, and what would the circumstances be? For example, would you have sex with someone for $1,000? How about for $1 million? Would you have to know the person beforehand?

*W*hat do you plan to tell
your children about sex, and
how old will they be before
you discuss the topic with
them? How important do
you think sex education is?

*W*hat is your favorite time
of day for sex? Why do
you prefer to have sex at
this time?

*I*s there any particular place where you would like to have sex? Have you ever had sex outside, on a beach, or in the woods? What's your favorite room in the house for having sex?

Would you ever pose nude for a magazine or star in a porno movie? What are your thoughts on pornography? Do you think it's a useful sexual aid? When, if ever, do you feel pornographers take things too far?

After years of imagining and wondering, did you feel disappointed the first time you had sex? What were your thoughts and your reaction immediately after your first sexual experience? How did the actual event compare and contrast with your daydreams before having sex for the first time?

Have you ever had a sexual experience with someone who had an STD? How did this experience affect you? Have you ever been treated for an STD? If so, how has this affected your life? What have you learned from this experience?

How did you feel after we had sex for the first time? What do you remember about that day? Was it perfect, or do you wish we had done anything differently?

Have you ever had sex with more than one person at the same time? Would you consider doing it again, or would you choose not to repeat the experience?

$\mathcal{D}$o you think that penis or breast size are important elements in successful sex? What experience do you have that makes you feel this way?

$\mathcal{T}$ell me about a sexual experience that you've had which was awkward or embarrassing. Was this situation avoidable? Do you fear that it will occur again in the future?

How do you feel about birth control? Does using a condom affect your enjoyment of sex? How have your feelings about birth control changed since you first began having sex?

What is my best talent in bed? Why do you like having sex with me, in particular?

Do you think sex changes after a couple is together for a long time? Do you think it changes after babies are born? If so, are you looking forward to these changes or do you believe they will have a negative affect on your sex life in the future?

If we were to expand our sexual horizons, what do you think we should try next? Is there anything that you would be too nervous to try in bed?

Have you ever been
shocked by either the participants or the scenario of one
of your sexual fantasies or
dreams? In retrospect, does
the fantasy or dream still
turn you on, or make sense
to you?

What makes you feel sexy? Is there an outfit that you wear, or a song that you hear that puts you in the mood? Are you sometimes surprised by your sexual feelings, or are they usually predictable?

*A*re you more interested in sex at this point in your life, or were you much more focused on it at an earlier stage? Would you prefer to make sex a more important part of your life in the near future, or are you satisfied with the state of your sex life?

*W*hat is missing from our sex life? Would you enjoy it if I were more spontaneous, or more eager to have sex at times? Do you wish we acted out fantasies, or tried to have sex in different positions and places?

$\mathscr{I}$s there anything that you would rather do than have sex? For example, if you had to choose between an afternoon in an art gallery with your favorite exhibits/at a meal with all of your favorite foods/at a party with all of your best friends/at a club with your favorite musician or an afternoon of sex, which would you pick?

About the Authors

D r. Michael J. Beck was educated at St. John's University, where he received his B.S. and his Ph.D. in psychology. He is a frequent contributor to numerous professional journals, including the Journal of Marital and Family Therapy, and the Journal of Counseling and Psychotherapy. Dr. Beck has also contributed chapters to a number of critically acclaimed books in the field, such as *Questions and Answers in Family Therapy*. He edited *The Narcissistic Family Member: Aspects of Development and Treatment* and served on the editorial board of the Journal of Hospital Psychiatry.

Though his main areas of concentration are couples and family treatment, Dr. Beck leads workshops and groups on a variety of topics. He is the president of The Babylon Consultation Center. In his free time, he enjoys boating, bird watching, and relaxing with his wife and children. His thirty years of marriage, and twenty-five child-filled years, have taught him a great deal about asking and answering all kinds of questions!

Stanis Marusak Beck is the Clinical Supervising Social Worker at the Babylon Consultation Center, where she has been practicing for more than fifteen years. She received her M.S.W. at Fordham University Graduate School of Social Service and post-graduate training at the Center for Modern Psychoanalytic Studies. She was awarded a certificate in Mediation from Columbia University and is currently pursuing an advanced degree in Mediation.

Ms. Beck is also interested in community organization and environmental issues, and writes a weekly environmental column for the local paper. She is the proud mother of two wonderful girls.

Seanna Beck is a graduate of Vassar College, where she studied English literature and creative writing. She is currently attending law school and plans to pursue a career in International Law. She enjoys cooking, travel, exploring New York City, and tormenting friends with endless questions.